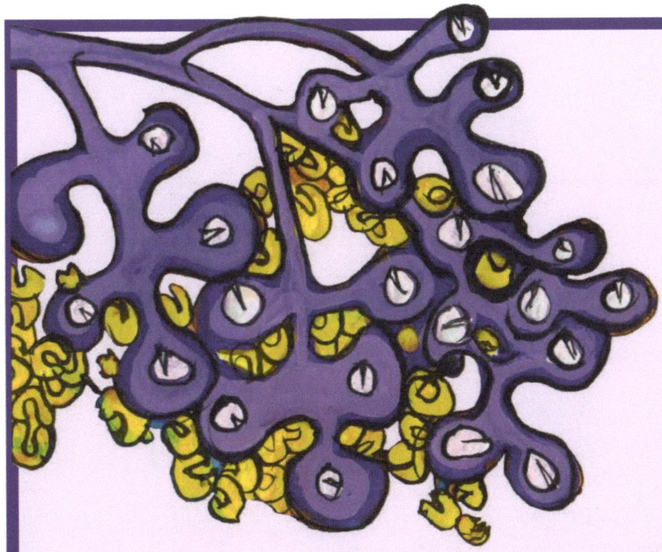

# Dinosaur Dreaming.

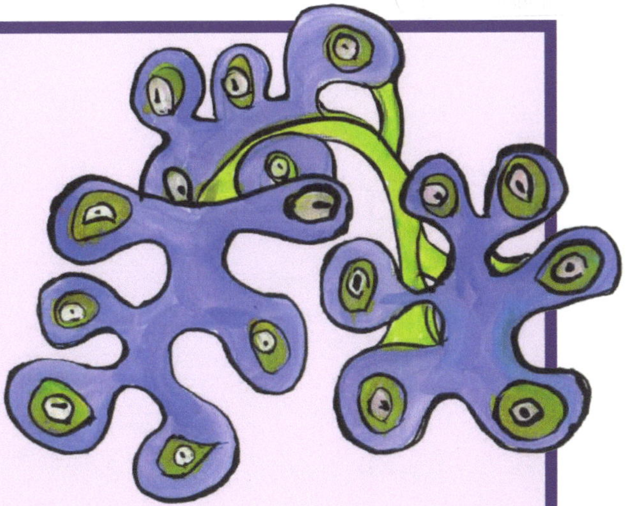

Written by

**Maureen LARTER**

Illustrated by

**Annie GABRIEL.**

©2019

Copyright © 2019 by Maureen Larter.

First published 2019. By Sweetfields Publishing
956 Comboyne Rd, Cedar Party, NSW Australia 2429

email: maureenlarter@gmail.com
blog :- readeatdream.net
twitter:- @maureenlarter
facebook:- www.facebook.com/BooksbyMaureenLarter

ISBN:- 978-0-6485076-4-2

A catalogue record for this book is available from
The National Library of Australia, Canberra, ACT, Australia

Set in Verdana font by Maureen Larter, Cedar Party, NSW, Australia.
Illustrations © 2019 by Annie Gabriel

## Other books written by Maureen:

### Little Words of Wisdom.

The soil

### Gardening Guides
- Summer
- Autumn
- Winter
- Spring
- Yearly guide

### Adult Drama

### (under the pen-name Marguerite Wellbourne)

Tarnished Gems
Ordeal by Innocence

### Business (How to) Booklet

The Start of Something Big

### Short Stories
- Book 1 - At the Beach - (4 stories)
- Book 2 – Predicaments – (5 stories)

### Books for young children

### Fairies from Aurora Village Series
1. Broken Wing.
2. Spiders, Lizards and Flies
3. Cave of the Golden Bower Bird

### For Toddlers

What about Me?
Arabella's Tree

### Alphabet Animals of Australia Series

- Angus Ant and the Acrobats
- Betty Bee's Birthday Bash
- Ben Brolga's Band
- Candy Cow and the Caterpillar
- Cassie Crocodile Catches a Cold
- Dorothy Dog and the Dangerous Dragonfly.
- Evie Emu's Encounter
- Frank Frog Feels Foolish
- Giddy the Galah
- Helen Heron and the Helicopter
- Iggy Ibis is Important
- John Jabiru and the Jolly Jam tin
- Kathy Koala's Kerfuffle
- Larry Lyrebird Laughs

This is an ongoing series. There are many more to come.

### Other chapter books for middle school children

Petey - Missing the Migration (book one)
In search of the Elusive Panda (A Kathy Edwards Adventure - book one)
Rosferado - Wizard extraordinaire.(book one)

## About the Author

**Maureen Larter** was born in England in the late 1940's and came over to Australia when still a toddler. She is a teacher of piano and violin, and lives on the lower Mid North Coast of New South Wales, Australia. She lives on a small-holding of 12 acres, and does her best to live self-sufficiently, while taking care of the soil and the environment. In the past, she has taught English, Social Studies, Music and Mathematics in High Schools within Australia, as well as living in China for a short time, teaching English.

On wet days, when she can't be out in her garden, and there are no students commandeering her time, she loves to sit and write. She writes children's stories and short stories, as well as occasional articles for magazines.

## About the Illustrator

**Annie Gabriel** is an illustrator, textile artist and book artist, who comes from a background of art and primary education. From an early age, she was constantly drawing and painting. One of her first inspirations was a book called 'The Little Brown Mouse". The little girl in the story painted her friend, the mouse, and so Annie began painting mice, too. As they say – the rest is history!

These days, Annie makes 'one-off' books for her grandchildren, and teaches them about art when they visit. Inspiration can strike at any time, and any place, and the art work for the stories by Maureen Larter are always a pleasure to create.

Other books illustrated by Annie:-

**Children's picture books:-**
What about me?
Arabella's Tree
**'Alphabet Animals of Australia' series**
Cassie Crocodile Catches a Cold
Dorothy Dog and the Dangerous Dragonfly
Giddy the Galah
Helen Heron and the Helicopter
Iggy Ibis is Important
John Jabiru and the Jolly Jam tin.
Kathy Koala's Kerfuffle
Children's Chapter books:-
**'Fairies of Aurora Village' series**
Broken Wing
Spiders, Lizards and Flies
Cave of the Golden Bower Bird

**There I was staring at a group of dinosaurs.**

**A Brontosaurus sauntered up, grazing on the treetops.**

**He was so big, and I thought he might tread on me, but he dropped his head down level with me and looked at me with his beautiful brown eyes.**

He smiled.

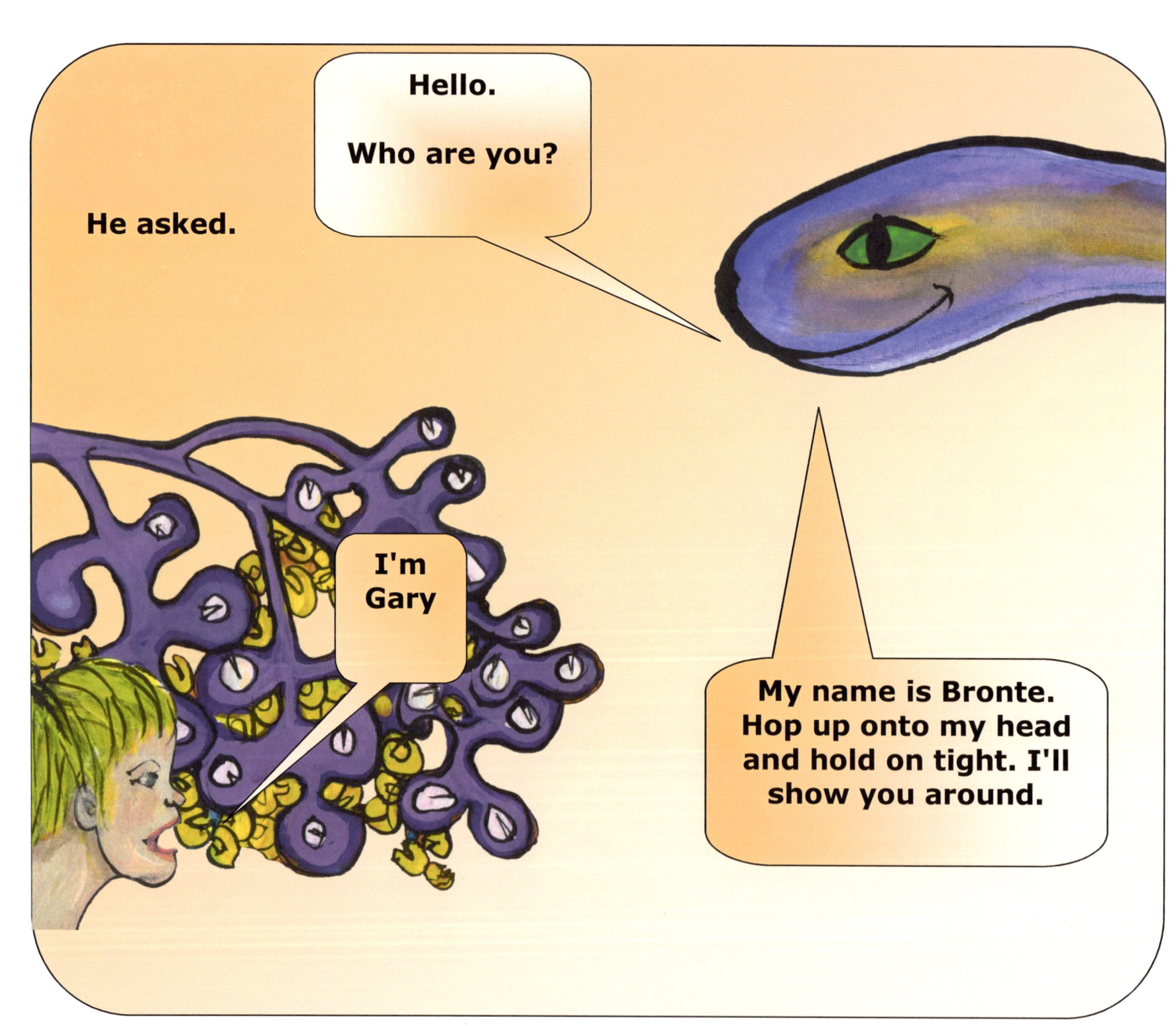

I wasn't frightened at all, so I got on and held on tightly. It was difficult, because his skin was hard to hold.

He lifted his head and my stomach flipped.

It was very high, but the view was impressive. After a few minutes I felt a little woozy, so I asked to be put down. I could see more and more trees, and lots of exciting things to see. He put his head down and I slipped gratefully down onto the ground.

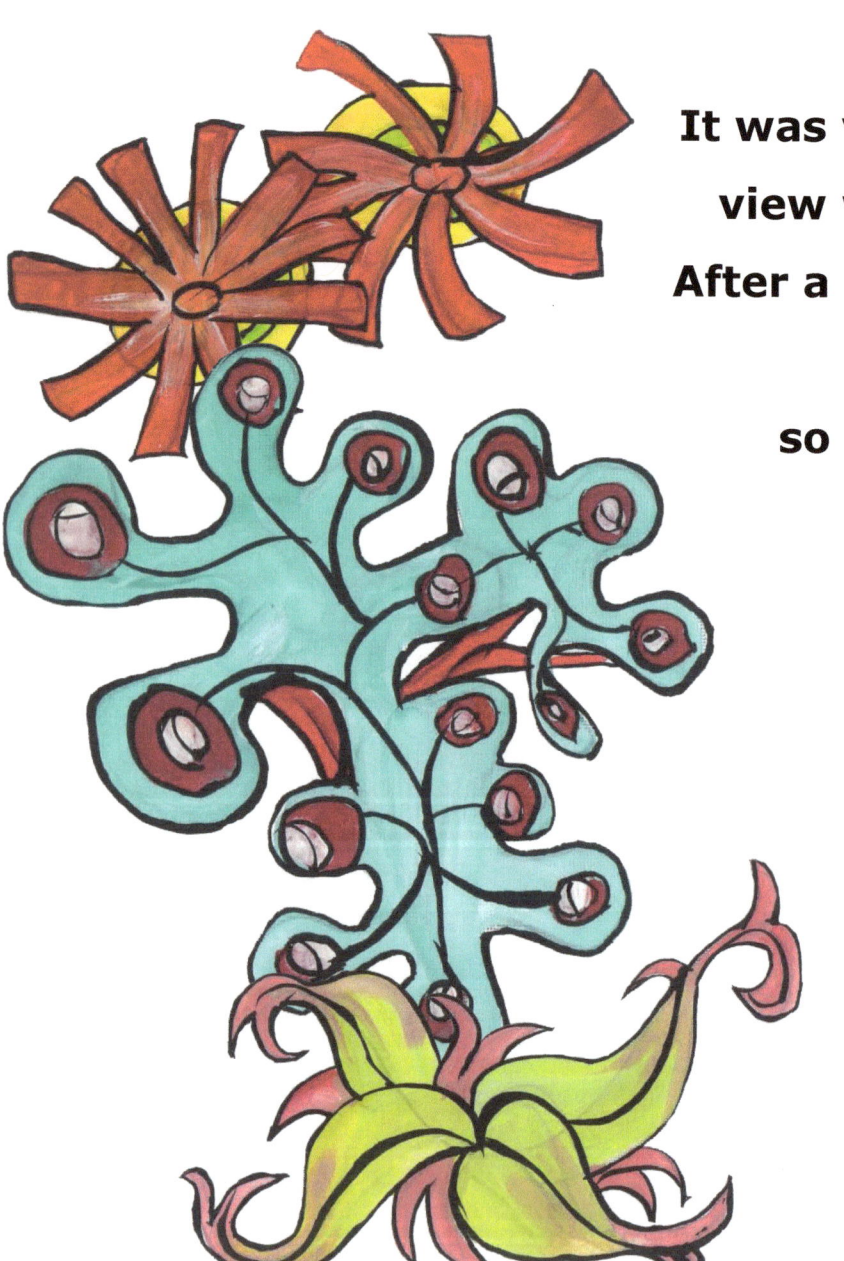

**Bronte lumbered off and I walked into the forest.**

In a clearing, I came to a halt.
I could see several Stegosaurus,
so I hid behind a plant.
One of them saw me and came over to me.
I was scared but he was friendly.

"Jump up on my head," he said "and I'll take you for a ride."

It was uncomfortable among his spines, so I decided to jump off.

Suddenly the herd of stegosaurus began to run and I had to hang on tight.

**A Raptor came running past and I leapt onto its back.**

**Not a moment too soon.**

**Out of the forest came a Tyrannosaurus Rex.**

He was roaring loudly.

**The Raptor ran and ran.**

**I bumped and shook.**

**I jostled and jolted.**

**Then the raptor leapt high and I fell off.**

**I flew up into the air.**

There was a big bump as I landed, and I opened my eyes.
I was back in my bed - and not a dinosaur in sight.

## **Projects for Schools.**

1. Find out about all different types of dinosaurs.
2. Can you be an archeologist and find some bones? Research a good place to try and go on an excursion to a river bed nearby.
3. Dress up as dinosaurs and have a fete day to collect funds for the school. Invite the parents and friends to a 'dinosaur feast' (Hint - make cakes in the shape of leaves and bones).
4. Do a project on one of the dinosaurs in this book.
5. How did dinosaurs become extinct? Study the history of our planet.
6. Go to a natural life museum, if there is one close to your school.
7. Study the planets, stars and Universe.
8. Watch a Professor Brian Cox video about all the planets, or a David Attenborough video about the animals on our planet.

Written
by
Maureen Larter

Illustrated
by
Annie Gabriel

©2019

www.ingramcontent.com/pod-product-compliance
Lightning Source LLC
Chambersburg PA
CBHW041327290426
44110CB00004B/158